Pupil's
Book
3
with Digital Pack

Pippa and Pop

British English

Caroline Nixon & Michael Tomlinson

with Lesley Koustaff & Susan Rivers

T0384660

CAMBRIDGE
UNIVERSITY PRESS

Map of the book

	VOCABULARY	LANGUAGE	SOUNDS AND LETTERS	LITERACY AND VALUES	NUMBERS	CROSS-CURRICULAR	PROJECT
Introduction Page 4							
1 Me! Page 6	Review Level 2: characters, numbers , likes *angry, bored, excited, scared, sleepy, surprised*	*Hello! What's your name? I'm (Kim).* *How old are you? I'm (eight).* *I like (books).* *What's her / his name?* *She's (Kim). He's (Dan).* *How old is she / he?* *She's / He's (eight).* *He's / She's / I'm (bored).* *He isn't / She isn't / I'm not (bored).*	Review Level 2 letter sounds: *b, m, t, g, p, d, k, n, s, h*	*Jane's name* Be yourself	Review numbers: *1 – 20*	Music: Emotions from music	Make a self portrait
2 My day Page 18	*brush my hair, brush my teeth, get dressed, have breakfast, wake up, wash my face* *go to bed, have a bath, have dinner, have a snack, listen to a story, play with friends*	*I (wake up) (in the morning / every day).* *They / We (play with friends) (after school / in the evening).* *We / They don't (have a bath).*	Letter sound /ʃ/ (sh)	*Brush your hair, Leo!* Look after yourself	Adding up by counting	Social studies: Times of day	Make a daily activities display
3 My home Page 30	*make the bed, pick up the toys, set the table, sweep the floor, wash the clothes, wash the dishes* *bed, bookcase, cupboard, lamp, rug, toy box*	*He / She (washes the dishes).* *I (sweep the floor).* *It's (under / in / on / next to) the (bed).*	Letter sound /k/ (ck)	*Goldilocks and the three bears* Respect other people's things	Numbers: *10, 20, 30, 40*	Social studies: Objects at home	Make and decorate a bedroom
Units 1–3 Review Page 42–43							
4 My sports Page 44	*badminton, baseball, basketball, football, hockey, tennis* *bouncing, catching, hitting, kicking, rolling, throwing*	*They're / She's / He's playing (football) .* *She's / He's / They're / I'm (throwing) the ball.*	Letter sound /ŋ/ (ng)	*A sport for Grace* Persevere	Subtracting by counting	Physical education: Team sports	Make a ball

	VOCABULARY	LANGUAGE	SOUNDS AND LETTERS	LITERACY AND VALUES	NUMBERS	CROSS-CURRICULAR	PROJECT
5 **My free time** Page 56	cooking dinner, drawing pictures, listening to music, playing video games, reading books, watching TV go roller skating, go swimming, play a board game, play with building blocks, play hide-and-seek, play outside	I / We like (reading books). Let's (go swimming / play a board game)! Can I (come / play)?	Letter sounds / ʊ / (short oo) and / uː / (long oo)	Jack loves reading Join in and help	Numbers: 50, 60	Art: Paintings, photographs and sculptures	Make a board game
6 **My food** Page 68	cake, chocolate, crisps, grapes, pineapple, sweets beans, cereal, fruit, meat, rice, vegetables	Would you like some (chocolate)? Yes, please. / No, thank you. I'd like some (sweets), please. I / We have (meat and rice) for (breakfast / lunch / dinner).	Letter sound / tʃ / (ch)	Share, Ricky Raccoon! Share	Estimating quantity	Science: Salty, sour and sweet	Make a plate of food
Units 4–6 Review Page 80–81							
7 **Animals** Page 82	crocodile, elephant, hippo, monkey, snake, tiger duck, giraffe, lizard, parrot, spider, zebra	There's (a monkey). There are (three) (monkeys). There are (lots of) (snakes). They're (giraffes). They've got (long necks / long legs / stripes / short legs / big feet / long tails / sharp teeth). They're (fast).	Letter sound / θ / (th)	The mouse and the lion Be friendly	Numbers: 70, 80	Science: Where animals live	Make an animal
8 **Plants** Page 94	garden, plants, rain, seeds, soil, sun beautiful, clean, dirty, new, old, ugly	What do plants need? Plants need (sun / rain / soil). What (beautiful) (flowers)! What (a dirty) (nose)!	Letter sound / iː / (ee, ea)	Sophia's garden Work together	Measuring length	Science: How plants grow	Make a plant diagram
9 **My town** Page 106	hospital, playground, restaurant, school, shop, supermarket doctor, farmer, nurse, shop assistant, teacher, waiter	Where are you / are we going? I'm / We're going to the (supermarket). A (teacher) works in a (school). He / She works on a farm. Where does (a teacher) work? Does (a nurse) work (in) a (hospital)? Yes, he / she does. No, he / she doesn't.	Letter sound / eɪ / (ay, ai)	Big-city cat and small-town cat Appreciate what you have	Numbers: 90, 100	Social studies: Jobs	Make a jobs poster
Units 7–9 Review Page 118–119							

Hello again!

HOSPITAL

Welcome back to *Pippa and Pop*

1 Me!

▶ 🎧³ **Listen to the song.**

to be ME!

1 Introduction and language review: *Hello! What's your name? I'm (Kim / Dan / Pippa / Pop / Tinks). How old are you? I'm (eight / five / six / three). I like (books / trains).*

🎧 Listen. 👆 Point. ⭕ Circle.

6　⑧

5　4

6　7

3　5

🎧 ⁵ Listen. ⭕ Stick. 📖 Match. 💬 Say.

1 **Language practice:** *What's your / her / his name? I'm / She's / He's (Kim / Dan / Pippa / Tinks). How old are you / is she / is he? I'm / She's / He's (eight / five / six / three).*

🎧6 **Listen.** ⭕ **Trace.** 📖 **Match.** 💬 **Say.**

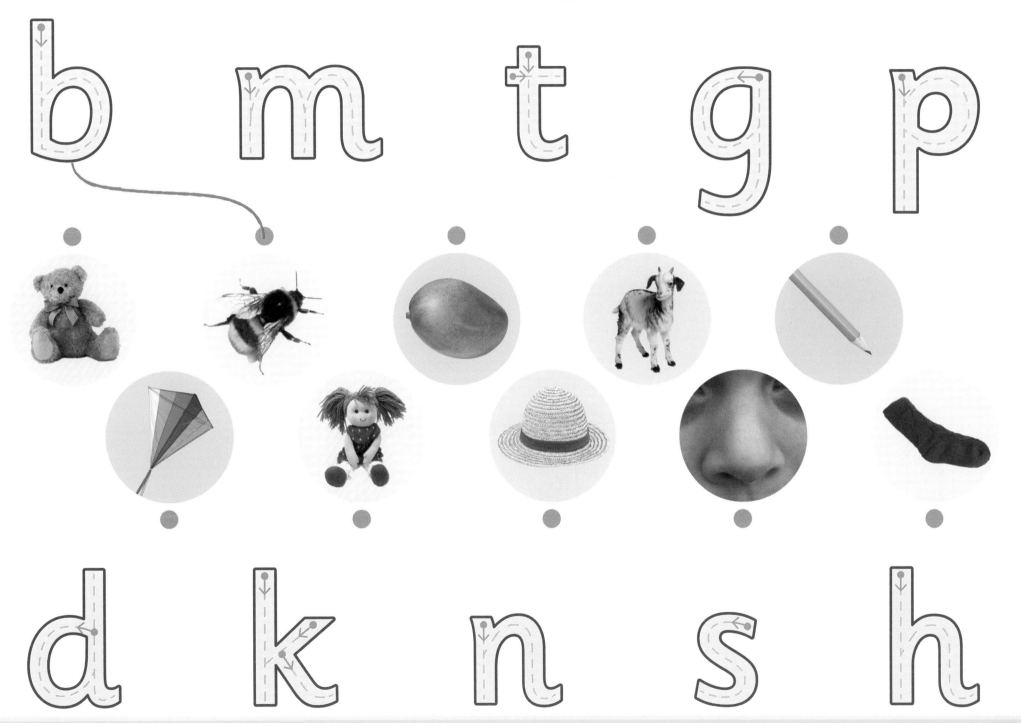

▶️ 🎧⁷ Listen. Jane's name

▶ 🎧⁸ Listen. ☝ Point. ⭕ Circle.

1 Language presentation: *He's / She's / I'm (bored / sleepy / surprised / angry / excited / scared). She isn't / He isn't / I'm not (bored).*

▶ 🎧⁹ **Listen.** 👁 **Look.** ⚪ **Circle.** 🎵 **Sing.**

👁 **Look.** ✋ **Count.** 📖 **Match.**

1 2 3 4	10	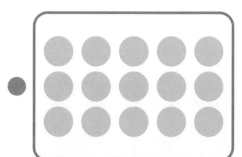
6 7 8 9	20	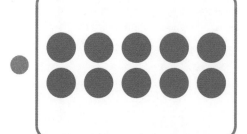
11 12 13 14	5	
16 17 18 19	15	

🎧 ¹⁰ Listen. ⭕ Circle.

1

2

3

 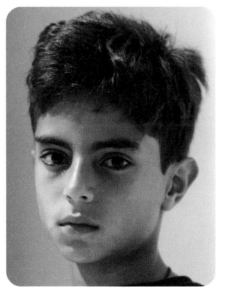

4

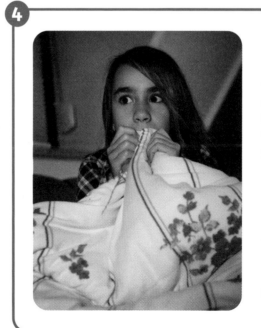 

🎧 ¹¹ **Listen.** ✏️ **Draw.** 💬 **Say.**

1 *He's / She's / I'm (bored / sleepy / surprised / angry / excited / scared). She isn't / He isn't / I'm not (bored).*

👁 **Look.** ✋ **Make.** 💬 **Say.**

What's (your) name? (I'm) (Ana). How old are you / is she / is he? I'm / She's / He's (five / six). **1** **17**

② My day

🎧 ¹³ Listen. 👆 Point. ⭕ Trace.

🎧 ¹⁴ Listen. ➡️➡️ Follow. ⬭ Stick. 💬 Say.

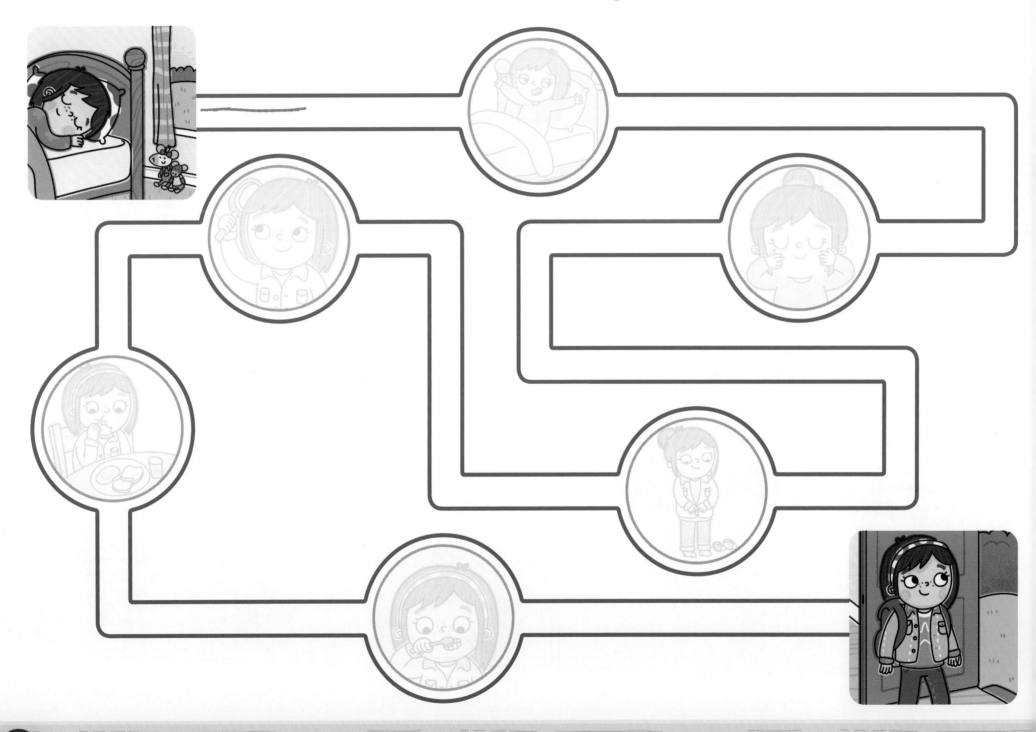

2 Language practice: *I (wake up / wash my face / get dressed / brush my hair / have breakfast / brush my teeth) every day.*

(15) 🎧 **Listen.** ⬭ **Trace.** ⬭ **Circle.** 💬 **Say.**

5

6

7

8

▶️ 🎧 17 Listen. 👆 Point. ⭕ Circle.

2 Language presentation: *They / We (play with friends / have a snack / have dinner / have a bath / listen to a story / go to bed) (after school / in the evening). We don't (have a bath).*

▶️ 🎧¹⁸ **Listen.** ✔️❌ **Tick or cross.** 🎵 **Sing.**

 **Count.** **Draw.** **Trace.** **Say.**

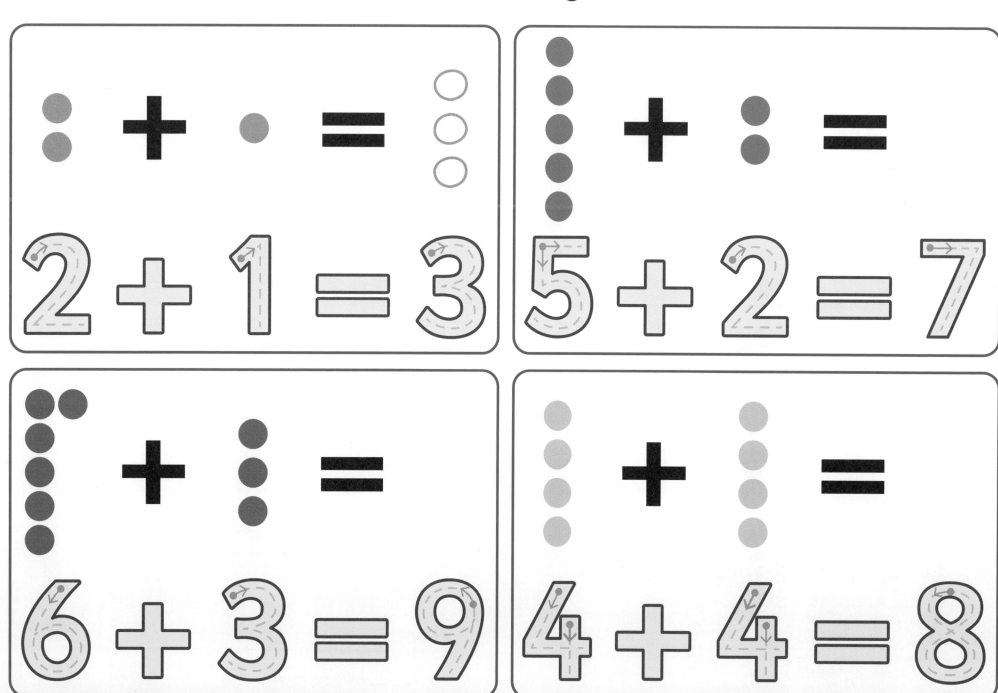

$2 + 1 = 3$

$5 + 2 = 7$

$6 + 3 = 9$

$4 + 4 = 8$

👁 Look. 📖 Match.

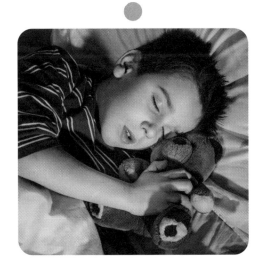

Review

🎧 **19** **Listen.** 📖 **Match.** 💬 **Say.**

2 *I (wash my face / get dressed / brush my hair / have breakfast / brush my teeth / listen to a story) (in the morning / every day / in the evening).*

👁 Look. 🙌 Make. 💬 Say.

③ My home

 Listen to the song.

🎧²¹ Listen. 👆 Point. ⭕ Circle.

🎧 ²² Listen. ⭕ Trace. 🔘 Stick. 💬 Say.

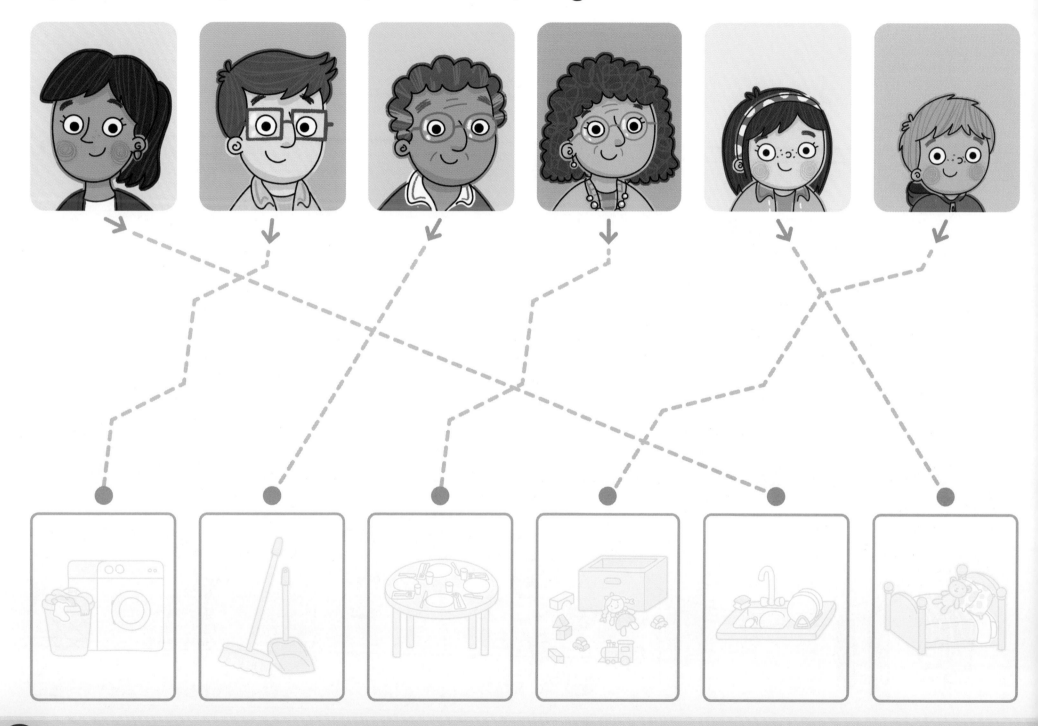

3 **Language practice:** *He / She (washes the dishes / sets the table / washes the clothes / makes the bed / sweeps the floor). I (pick up the toys).*

🎧 ²³ **Listen.** ⬭ **Trace.** ◯ **Circle.** 🗨 **Say.**

1

2

3

4

5

6

7

8

▶ 🎧²⁵ Listen. 👆 Point. ✏ Colour.

③ Language presentation: *It's (under / on / in / next to) the (bed / rug / cupboard / toy box / lamp / bookcase).*

▶️ 🎧²⁶ **Listen.** ✔️ ❌ **Tick or cross.** 🎵 **Sing.**

🎧²⁷ **Listen.** ⭕ **Trace.** ✋ **Count.** ✏️ **Colour.**

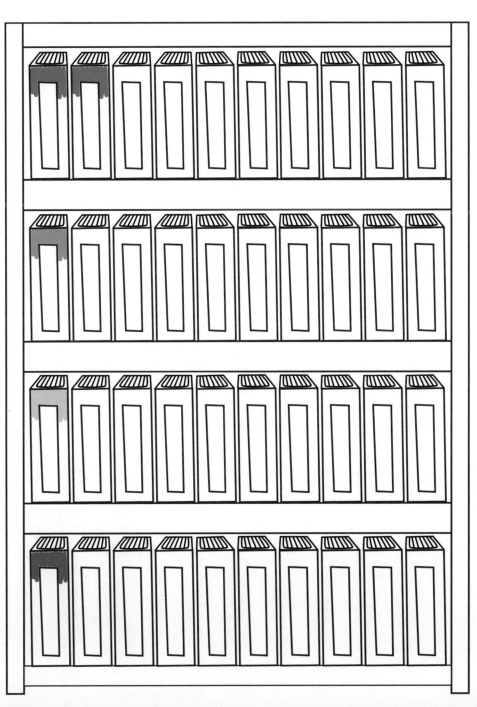

👁 Look. 📘 Match.

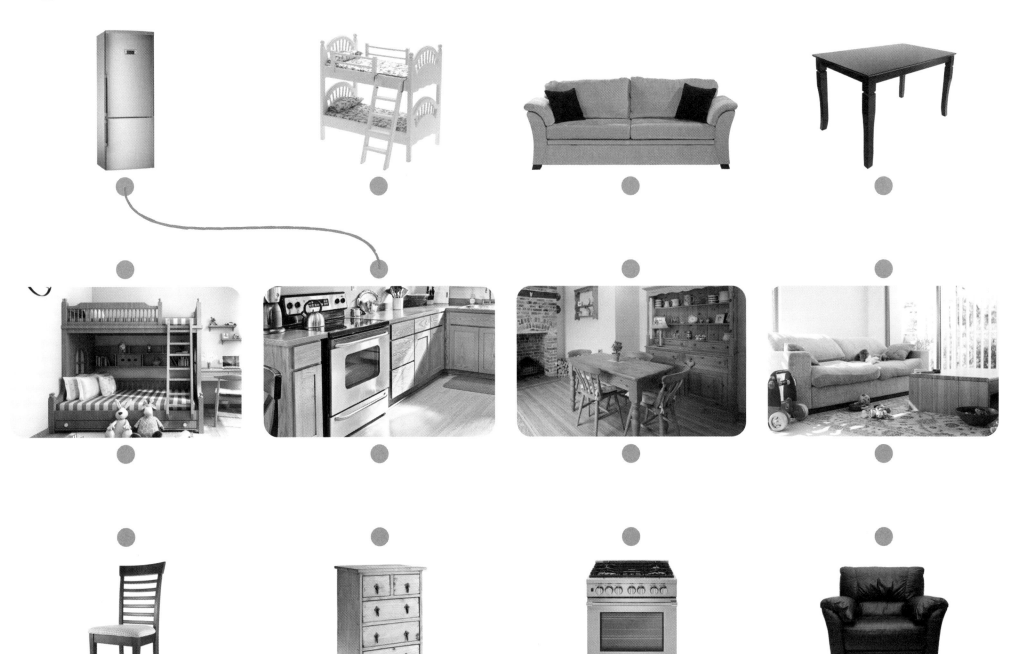

🎧²⁸ Listen. 📖 Match. 💬 Say.

3 *He / She (washes the dishes / picks up the toys / sets the table / washes the clothes / makes the beds / sweeps the floor) (in the morning).*

👁 Look. 🤲 Make. 💬 Say.

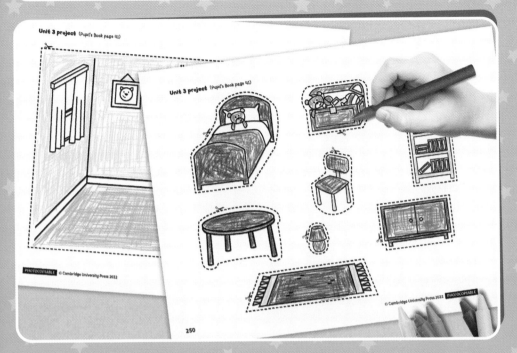

🎧 **29 Listen.** 🔍 **Find.** 123 **Number.** 💬 **Say.**

$4 + 2 =$ 6

$5 + 3 =$ ___

$10 + 1 =$ ___

$10 + 10 =$ ___

4 My sports

 🎧30 **Listen to the song.**

🎧³¹ Listen. 👆 Point. ¹²³ Number.

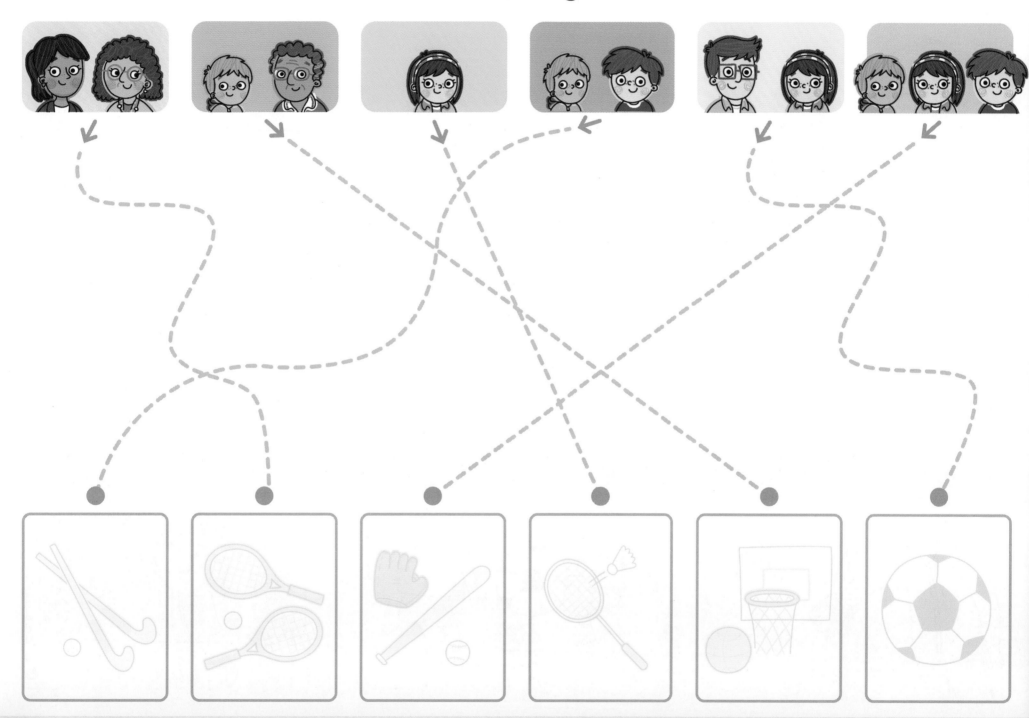

4 Language practice: *They're / She's / He's playing (football / badminton / tennis / baseball / hockey / basketball).*

🎧 **(33) Listen.** ⭕ **Trace.** ⭕ **Circle.** 💬 **Say.**

1

I'm bored.

2

I like sports.

3

I don't like basketball.

4

I don't like hockey.

Listen. Point. Circle.

4 Language presentation: *She's / He's / They're / I'm (throwing / hitting / catching / bouncing / rolling / kicking) the ball.*

▶ 🎧³⁶ **Listen.** 👁 **Look.** ○ **Circle.** 🎵 **Sing.**

✋ **Count.** ✏️ **Draw.** ⭕ **Trace.** 💬 **Say.**

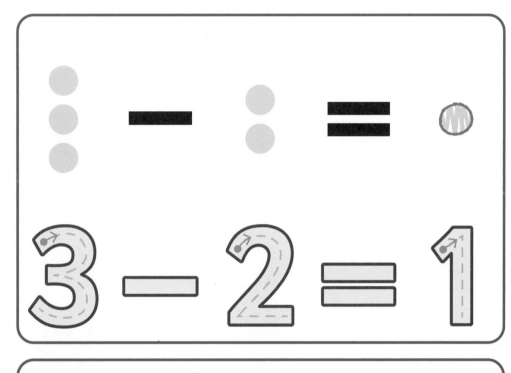

$3 - 2 = 1$

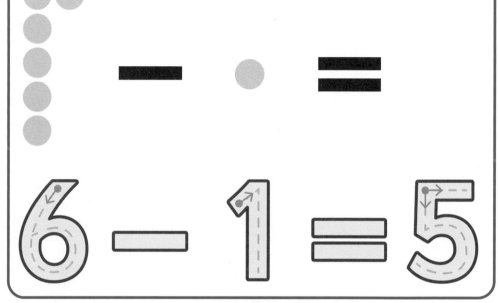

$6 - 1 = 5$

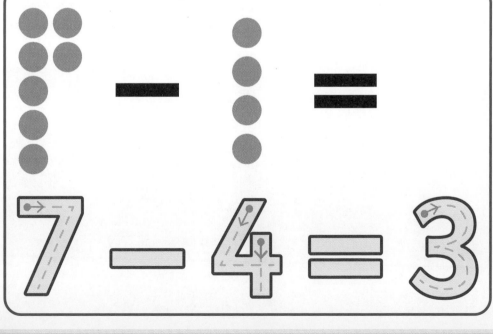

$7 - 4 = 3$

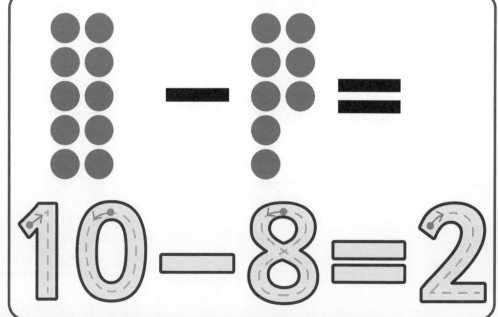

$10 - 8 = 2$

🎧 ₃₇ Listen. 📖 Match.

9

11

5

Review

🎧 (38) Listen. ✔ ✘ Tick or cross. 💬 Say.

1. ✔
2.
3.
4.
5.
6.
7.
8.

4 *They're / She's / He's playing (football / badminton / tennis / baseball / hockey / basketball). They're / She's / He's (throwing / hitting / catching / bouncing / rolling / kicking) the ball.*

👁 Look. 🖐 Make. 😊 Play.

5 My free time

5 **Unit topic introduction:** Free-time activities

🎧 Listen. 👆 Point. 123 Number.

🎧⁴¹ Listen. ⭕ Trace. 🔘 Stick. 💬 Say.

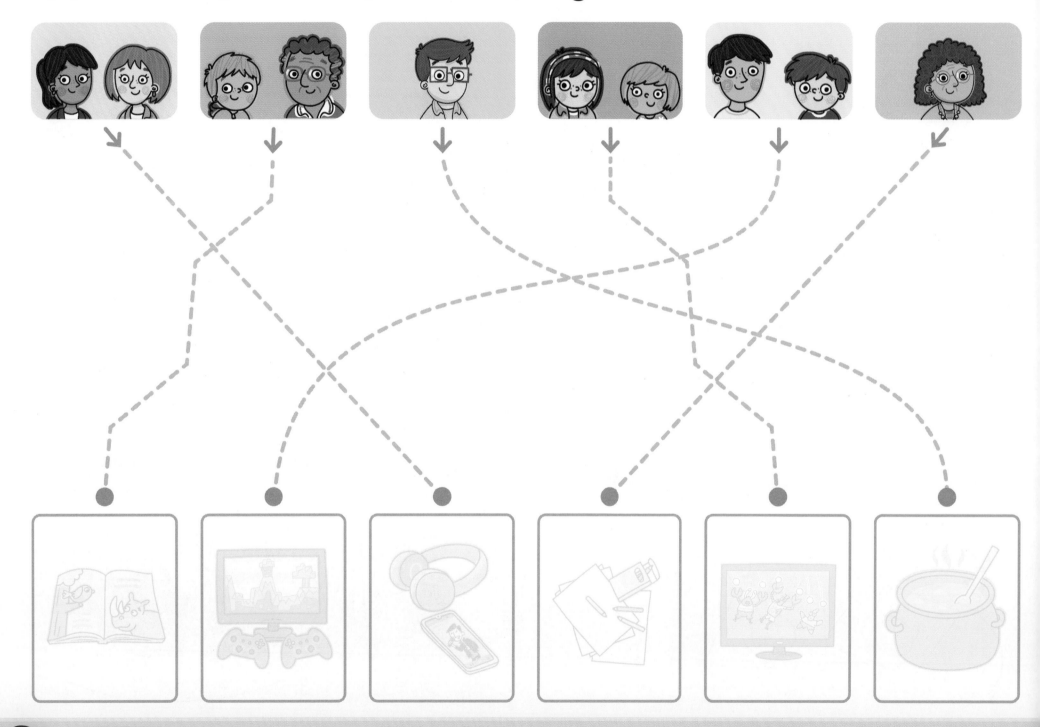

5 *Language practice: I / We like (reading books / cooking dinner / watching TV / playing video games / listening to music / drawing pictures).*

🎧 (42) **Listen.** ⭕ **Trace.** ⭕ **Circle.** 💬 **Say.**

▶️ 🎧 43 Listen. Jack loves reading

1

Jack likes reading books.

2

Jack likes superheroes.

3

4

Come and help, please.

1

2

3

4

5

6

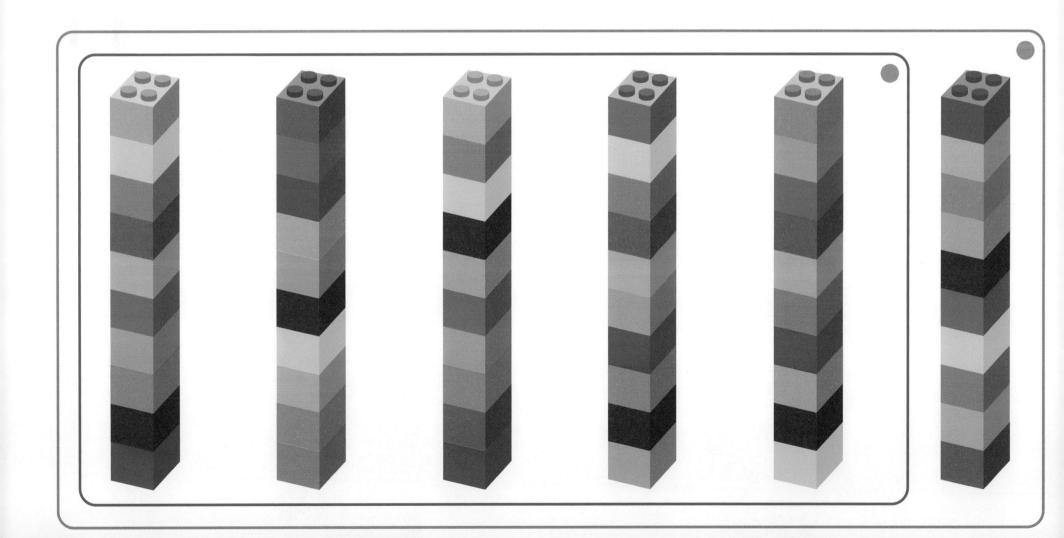

🎧 **Listen.** ⭕ **Trace.** ✋ **Count.** 📖 **Match.**

10 20 30 40 50 60

👁 Look. 📖 Match.

Listen. Number. Say.

1

5 *I / We like (reading books / cooking dinner / watching TV / playing video games / listening to music / drawing pictures).*

👁 Look. 🖐 Make. 😊 Play.

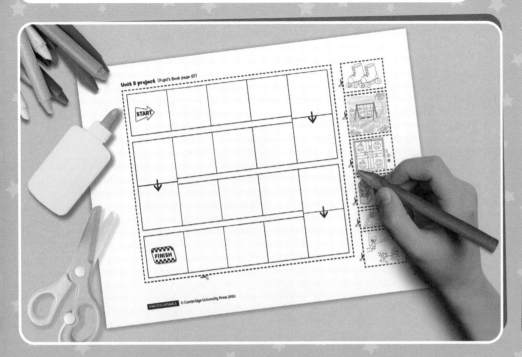

6 My food

 **Listen to the song.**

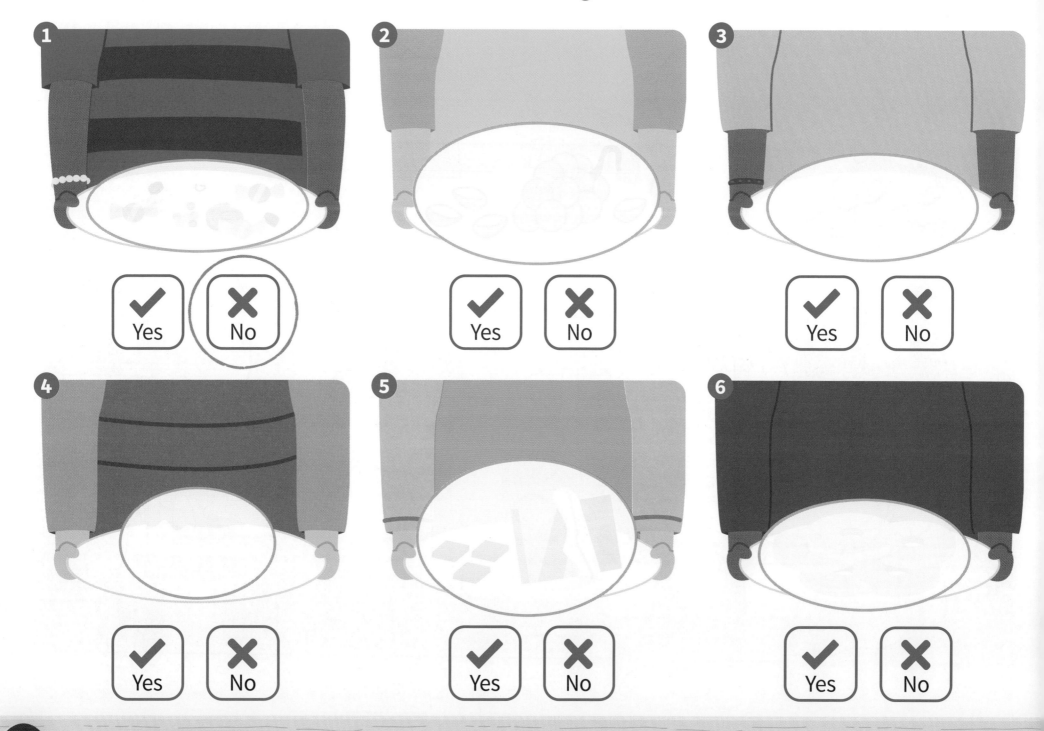

6 Language practice: *Would you like some (chocolate / grapes / crisps / sweets / pineapple / cake)? Yes, please. / No, thank you.*

🎧 ⁵¹ **Listen.** ◯ **Trace.** ✏️ **Colour.** 💬 **Say.**

Share, Ricky Raccoon!

Ricky is eating the sweets.

Ricky is eating the ice cream.

Where's our ice cream?

Ricky is eating the cake.

5 Where's my birthday cake?

6 Ricky is sad.

7 Let's make some biscuits.

8 Ricky is sharing!

6 Language presentation: *I / We have (meat / rice / fruit / cereal / vegetables / beans) for (breakfast / lunch / dinner).*

Listen. ✔ ✗ Tick or cross. ♫ Sing.

💬 **Say.** ⭕ **Circle.** ✋ **Count.** ✏️ **Write.**

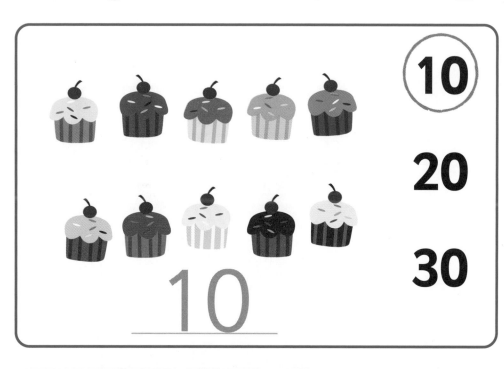

10

20

30

10

20

40

60

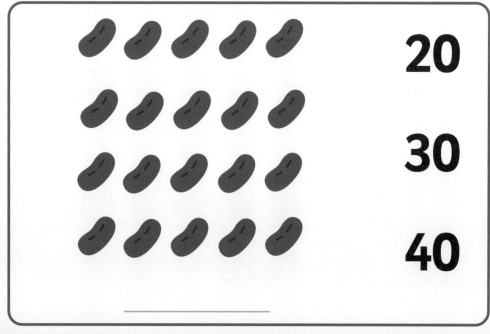

20

30

40

10

30

50

👁 **Look.** ◯ **Circle.**

salty

sour

sweet

🎧 55 Listen. 📖 Match. 💬 Say.

6 *Would you like some (chocolate / grapes / crisps / sweets / pineapple / cake)? Yes, please. / No, thank you. I'd like (lots of) grapes.*

👁 Look. 🙌 Make. 💬 Say.

🎧 56 **Listen.** 🔍 **Find.** 123 **Number.** 💬 **Say.**

👋 Count. ✏️ Draw. ✒️ Write.

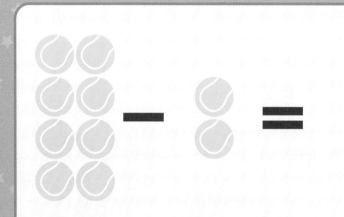

6 − 3 = *3*

8 − 2 = _____

10 − 7 = _____

9 − 5 = _____

7 Animals

 Listen. 👆 Point. 🔢 Number.

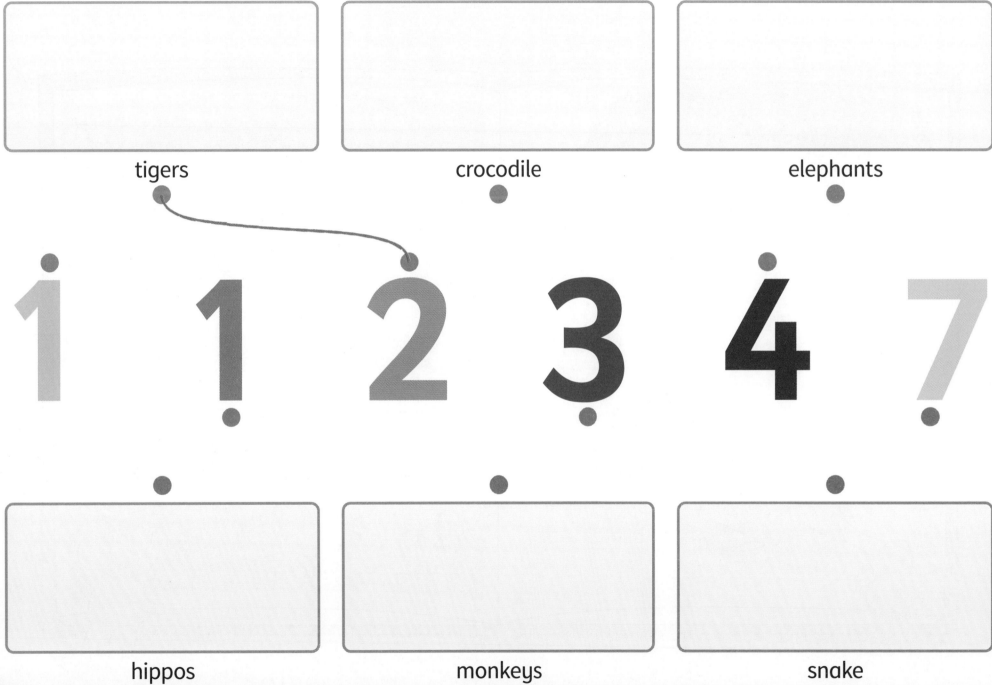

tigers

crocodile

elephants

1 1 2 3 4 7

hippos

monkeys

snake

7 **Language practice:** *There's (a crocodile / a snake). There are (two) (tigers / monkeys / hippos / elephants). There are lots of (monkeys).*

🎧 **Listen.** ⭕ **Trace.** ◯ **Circle.** 💬 **Say.**

1

The mouse sees a big lion.

2

I'm not scared!

3

I'm small. You're big.

4

The lion wakes up!

5

Don't be angry, Lion!

6

Let's be friends.

7

Can you help me?

8

You're a good friend.

1

Giraffes!

2

3

4

5

6

7 **Language presentation:** *They're (giraffes / zebras / ducks / parrots / lizards / spiders). They've got (long necks / long legs / stripes / short legs / big feet / long tails). They're (fast).*

▶️ 🎧 63 **Listen.** ⭕ **Trace.** ✏️ **Colour.** 🎵 **Sing.**

🎧 64 **Listen.** ⭕ **Trace.** ✋ **Count.** ✏️ **Colour.**

10 20 30 40 50 60 70 80

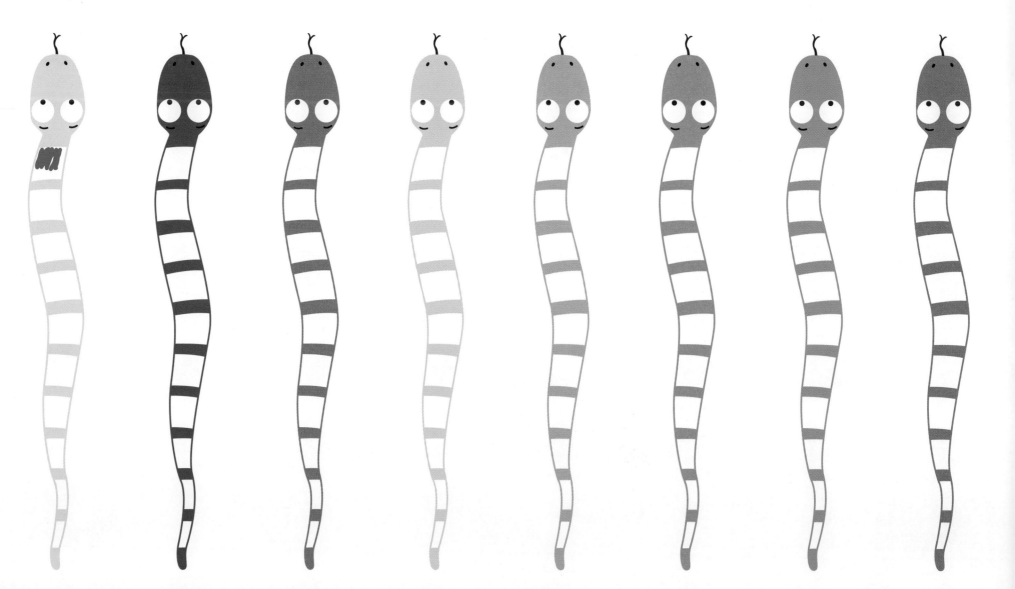

7 Numbers: *70, 80*

Science

🎧 **⁶⁵ Listen.** 👁 **Look.** 📖 **Match.**

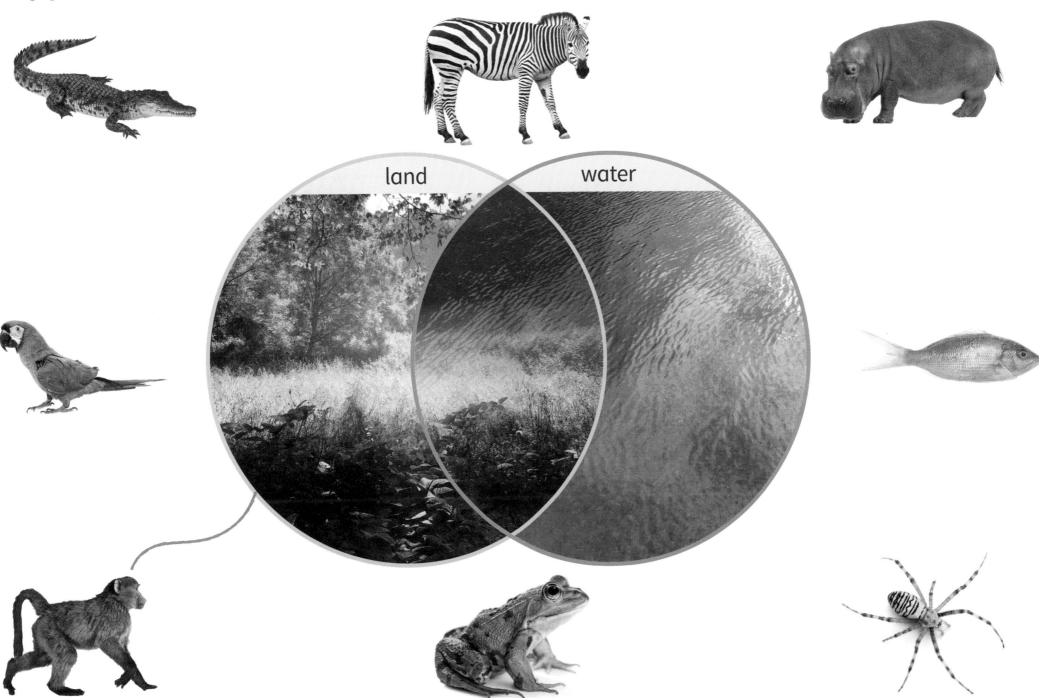

land   water

Review

🎧⁶⁶ Listen. ⭕ Circle. 💬 Say.

1

parrots

lizards

2

zebras

hippos

3

ducks

crocodiles

4

giraffes

elephants

7 *They're (giraffes / zebras / ducks / parrots / lizards / crocodiles / hippos / elephants). They've got (long necks / long legs / stripes / short legs / long tails / sharp teeth / small ears).*

👁 **Look.** 🖐 **Make.** 💬 **Say.**

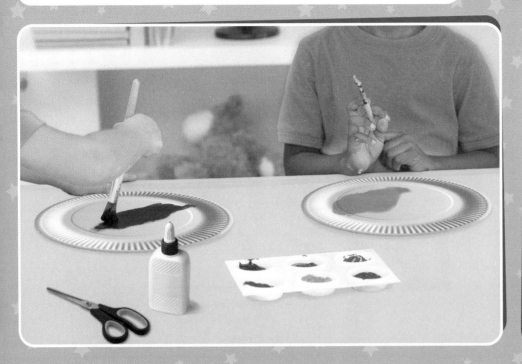

There's a (tiger / snake / spider). There are (four) (tigers). There are (lots of) (snakes). **7**

8 Plants

▶ 🎧 67 **Listen to the song.**

🎧 Listen. 👆 Point. 1️⃣2️⃣3️⃣ Number.

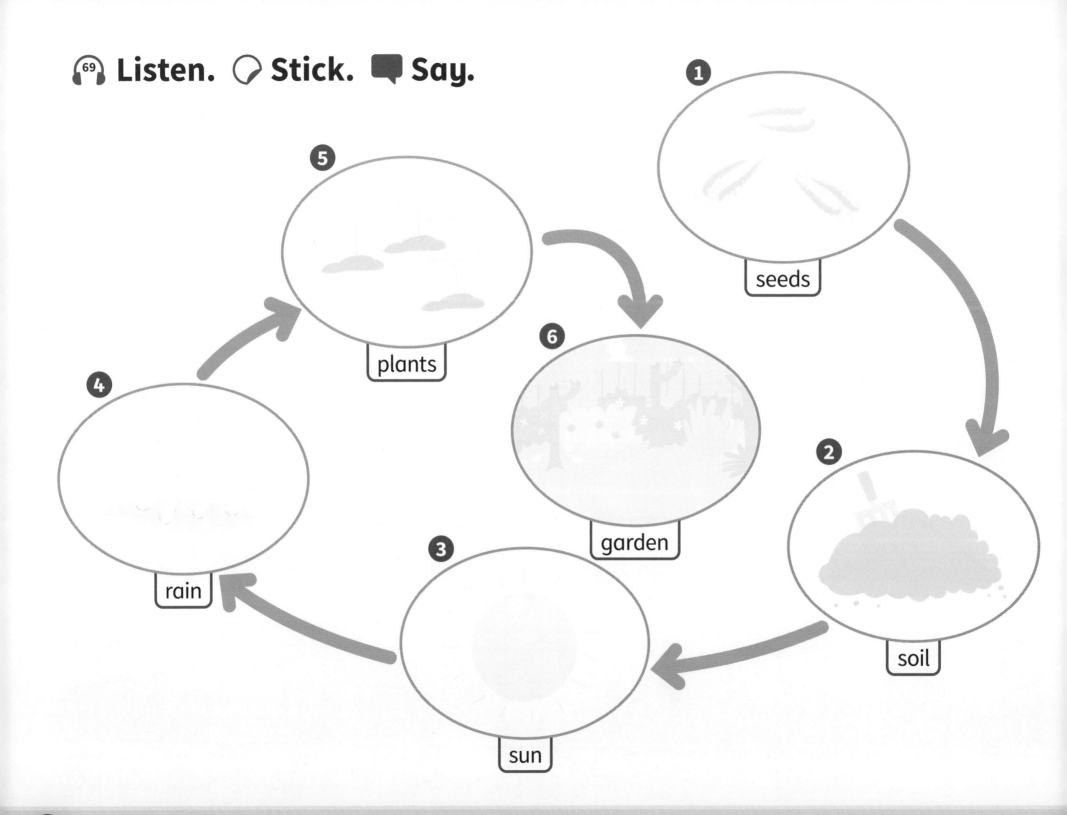

🎧 **Listen.** ⚪ **Stick.** 💬 **Say.**

1 seeds

5 plants

6 garden

4 rain

2 soil

3 sun

8 Language practice: *garden, seeds, plants, sun, rain, soil; Plants need (sun / rain / soil).*

🎧 70 **Listen.** ⬭ **Trace.** ◯ **Circle.** 💬 **Say.**

Sophia's garden

1

Sophia wants a garden.

2

The sun and the rain cloud are watching.

3

It rains and rains.

4

Plants need sun.

5

Plants need rain.

6

What a beautiful garden!

Sophia is sad.

7

Now the plants grow and grow.

8

What a beautiful garden!

What a dirty nose!

8 **Language presentation:** *beautiful, dirty, ugly, new, old, clean; What (beautiful) flowers! What (a dirty) (nose)!*

beautiful ✔

ugly

beautiful

dirty

new

new

old

dirty

clean

👁 **Look.** ✋ **Count.** ✏ **Write.**

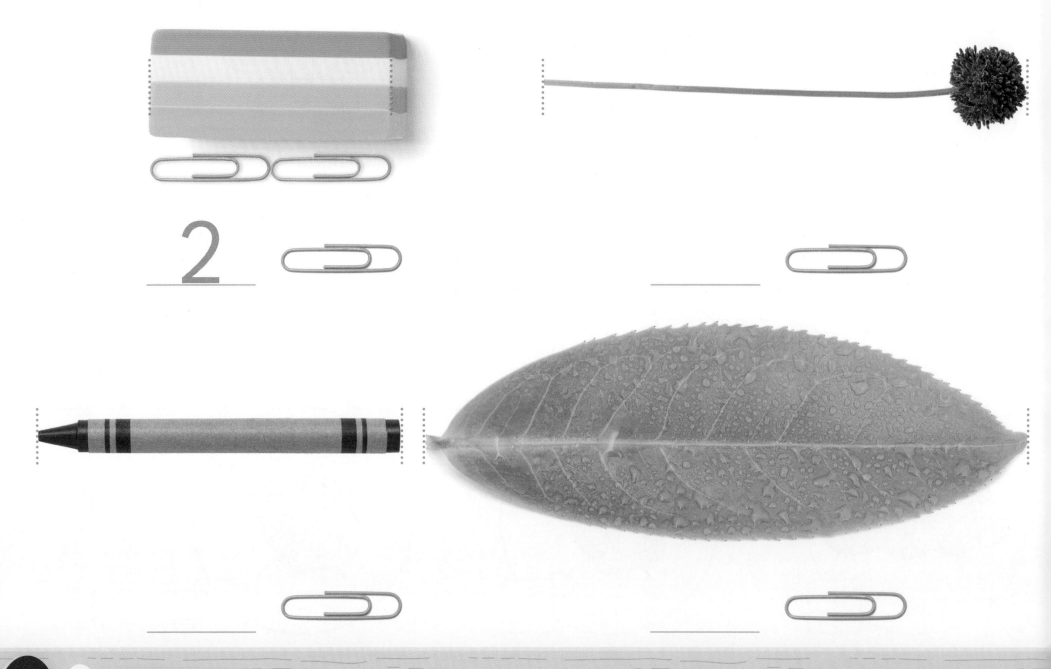

2

👁 Look. 1̤23 Number.

Review

8 *beautiful, dirty, ugly, new, old, clean; What (dirty) (hands)! What (an ugly) (beach)!*

👁 Look. 👐 Make. 💬 Say.

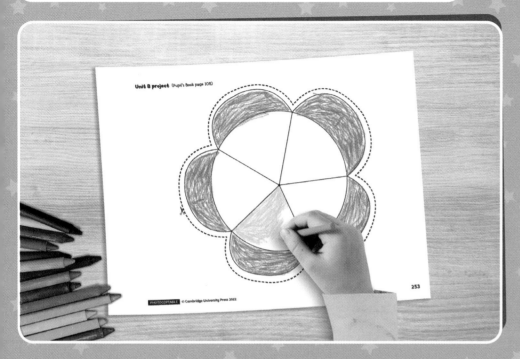

Plants need sun.

9 My town

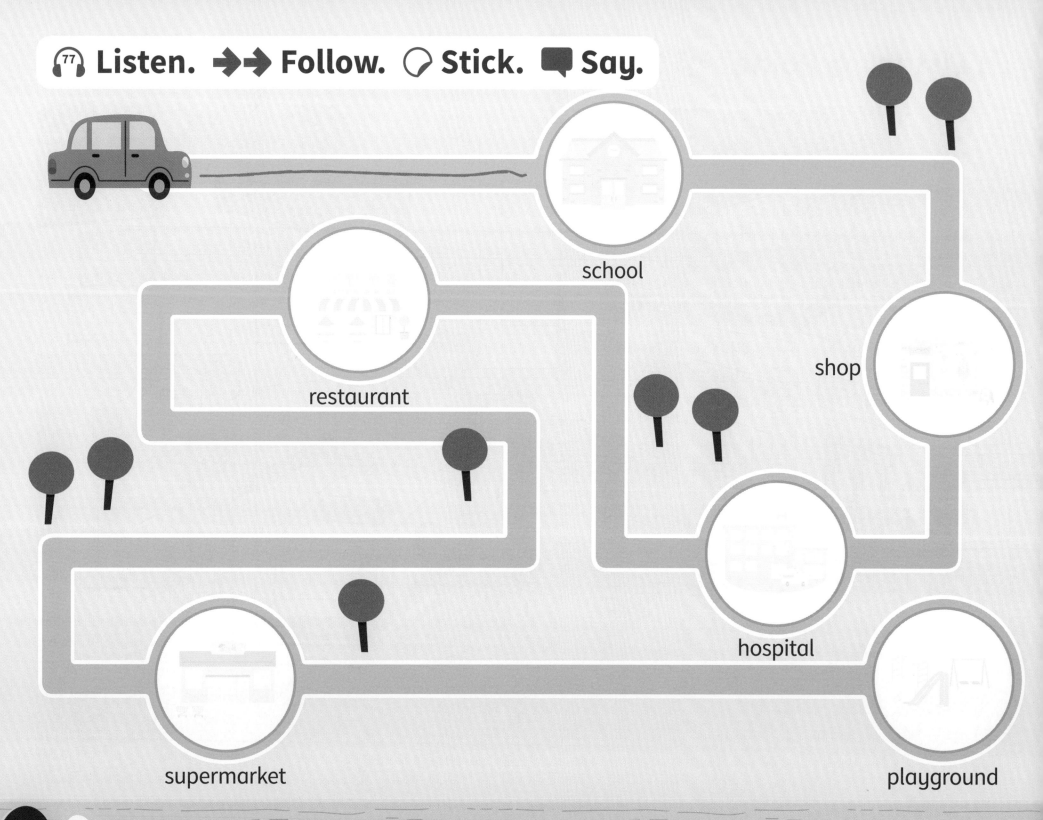

9 **Language practice:** *Where are we going? We're going to the (supermarket / restaurant / hospital / shop / school / playground).*

78 **Listen.** ⭕ **Trace.** ⭕ **Circle.** 💬 **Say.**

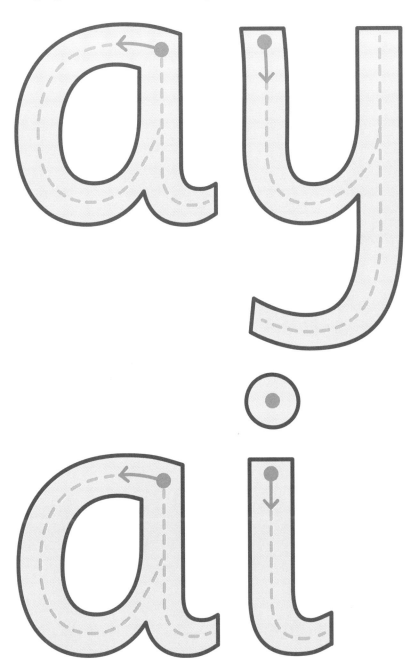

▶ 🎧(79) Listen. Big-city cat and small-town cat

Ben and Bill say goodbye.

1

A teacher works in a school.

2

3

4

5

6

▶️ 🎧 ⁸¹ **Listen.** 📓 **Match.** 🎵 **Sing.**

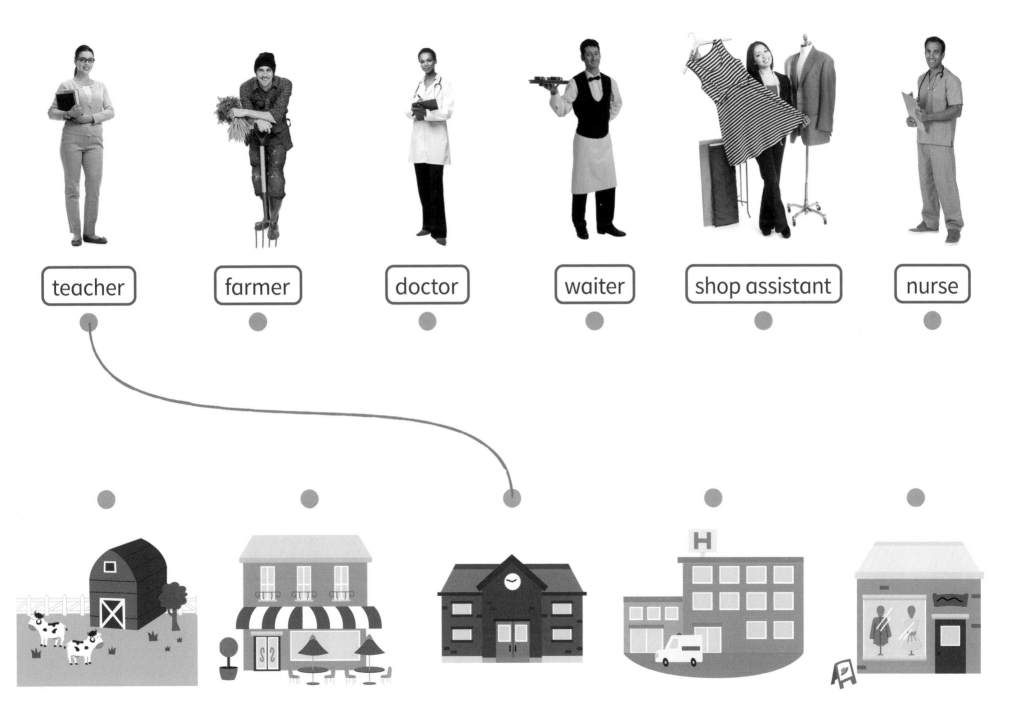

teacher   farmer   doctor   waiter   shop assistant   nurse

🎧 **82 Listen.** ⭕ **Trace.** ✋ **Count.** ✏️ **Colour.**

20   **40**   **60**   **80**   **100**

10   **30**   **50**   **70**   **90**

🎧 **Listen.** 👁 **Look.** ✔✘ **Tick or cross.**

Review

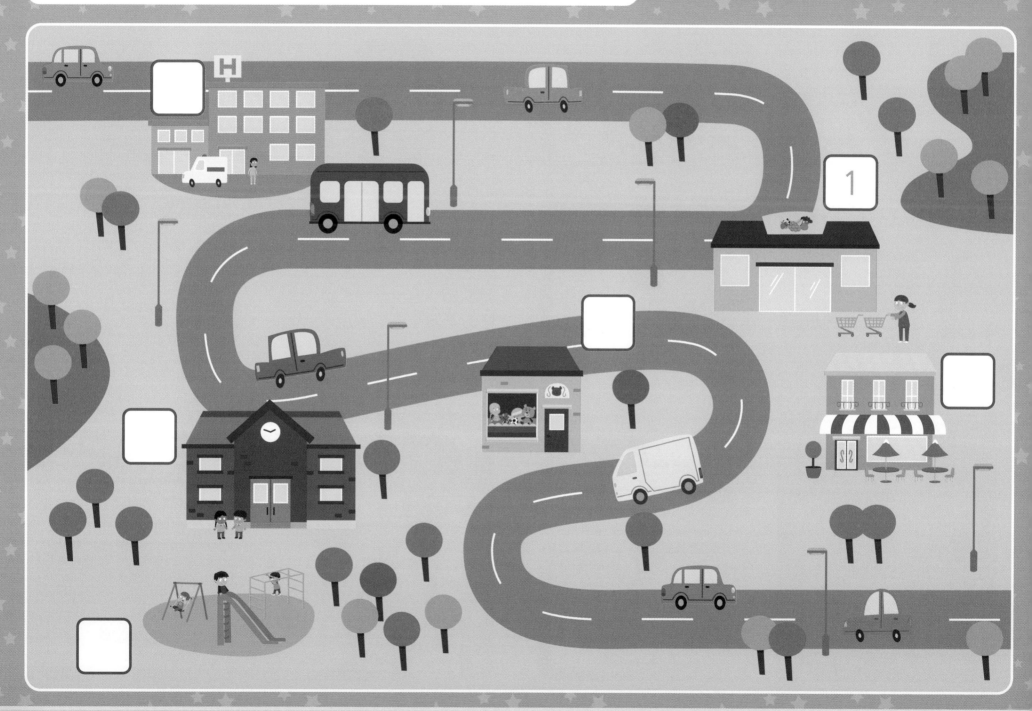

9 *Where are we going? We're going to the (supermarket / restaurant / hospital / shop / school / playground).*

👁 Look. 🖐 Make. 💬 Say.

Unit 9 project (Pupil's Book page 117)

A cook works in a restaurant.

A (cook / doctor) works in a (restaurant / hospital). A (farmer / bus driver) works on a (farm / bus). 9

🎧 85 Listen. 🔍 Find. 123 Number. 💬 Say.

1

👁 **Look.** ✋ **Count.** ◯ **Circle.**

20 🌱 40 🌷 60 100 🌰

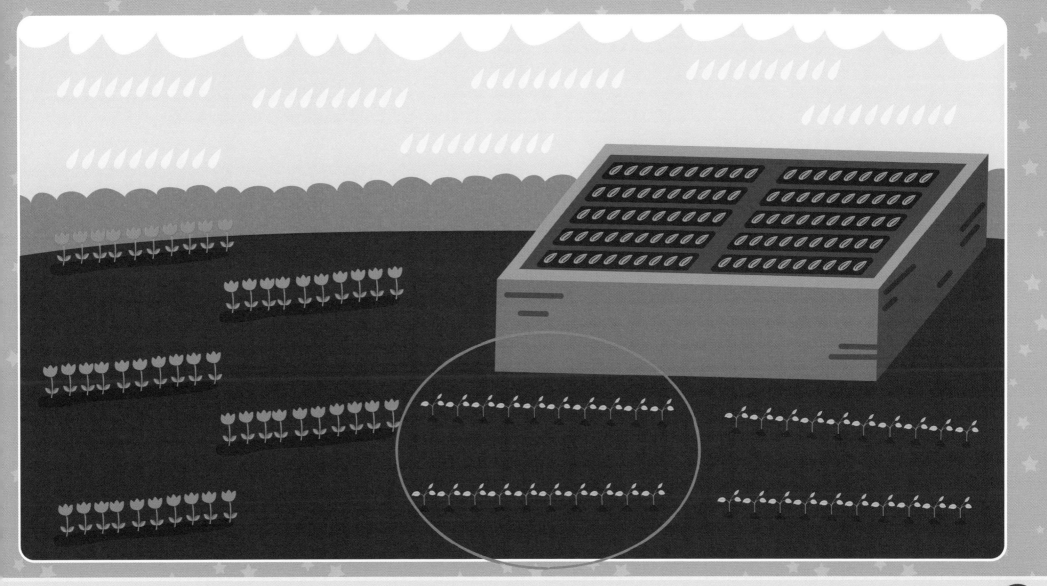

Thanks and Acknowledgements

Authors' thanks

Many thanks to everyone at Cambridge University Press for their dedication and hard work in extraordinarily complicated circumstances, and in particular to:

Liane Grainger for her unwavering professionalism and her irrepressible joviality;

Emily Hird for her endless enthusiasm, good humour and sound judgement;

Jane Holt for her unflagging energy and her ability to bring the whole, sprawling project together;

Vanessa Gold for her hard work and sound editorial contribution.

Catherine Ball and Carolyn Wright for their hard work helping to review, correct and knead the manuscript into shape.

Our thoughts and hearts go out to all the teachers and their pupils who have suffered and continue to suffer the devastating effects of the global pandemic that has changed all our lives. Stay strong.

Dedications

For Giuseppe Vincenti with love. The biggest and strongest heart I know. – CN

For Paloma, Pablo and Carlota, keep on smiling, love – MT

Caroline Nixon and Michael Tomlinson, Murcia, Spain

The publishers and authors would like to thank the following contributors:

Additional writing by Lesley Koustaff, Susan Rivers and Catherine Ball.

Book design and page make-up by Blooberry Design.

Cover design by Blooberry Design.

Commissioned photography by Blooberry Design.

Freelance editing by Catherine Ball, Amy Griggs and Carolyn Wright.

Audio recording and production by Ian Harker.

Original songs and chants by Robert Lee.

Songs and chants production by Jake Carter.

Animation production by QBS and Collaborate Agency.

The authors and publishers acknowledge the following sources of copyright material and are grateful for the permissions granted. While every effort has been made, it has not always been possible to identify the sources of all the material used, or to trace all copyright holders. If any omissions are brought to our notice, we will be happy to include the appropriate acknowledgements on reprinting and in the next update to the digital edition, as applicable.

Key: U = Unit.

Photography

All photos are sourced from Getty Images.

U1: Mike Kemp; FatCamera/E+; photosindia; Blurra/E+; Antagain/E+; Richard Newstead/Moment; FRANCOIS-EDMOND/iStock/Getty Images Plus; GlobalP/iStock/Getty Images Plus; kali9/E+; ElementalImaging/iStock/Getty Images Plus; PhotoAlto/Laurence Mouton/PhotoAlto Agency RF Collections; zayatssv/iStock/Getty Images Plus; Roland Magnusson/EyeEm; Nirut Punshiri/EyeEm; Jose Luis Pelaez Inc/Digital Vision; Imgorthand/E+; Lea Paterson/Science Photo Library; Caroline Schiff; Juanmonino/istock/Getty Images Plus; Westend 61; Ideabug/istock/Getty Images Plus; Asya_mix/iStock/Getty Images Plus; Lubushka/iStock/Getty Images Plus; Mai Vu/iStock/Getty Images Plus; antadi1332/iStock/Getty Images Plus; Irina_Strelnikova/iStock/Getty Images Plus; **U2:** JohnyGreig/E+; Kelvin Murray/Photodisc; ER productions limited/Digital vision; Corbis/VCG; Tetra Images; Damircudic/E+; Khilagan/iStock/Getty Images Plus; Sally Anascombe/Stone; PhotoNotebook/iStock/Getty Images Plus; JGI/Jamie Grill; Chris Hackett; Jose A. Bernat Bacete/Moment; Jiri V'aclavek/EyeEm; Kyoshino/istock/Getty Images Plus; Westend 61; Sean Locke/Photodisc; Jose Luis Pelaez Inc/Digital Vision; Deyangeorgiev/iStock/Getty Images Plus; Solstock/iStock/Getty Images Plus; Zubbin Shroof/The Image bank; Ariel Skelley/Digital Vision; Monkeybuisnessimages/iStock/Getty Images Plus; Image Source; eurobanks/iStock/Getty Images Plus; Elinamaninen/iStock/Getty Images Plus; Secret agent mike/moment; Serezniy/iStock/Getty Images Plus; Pictofoloia/E+; Asya_mix/iStock/Getty Images Plus; Lubushka/iStock/Getty Images Plus; Mai Vu/iStock/Getty Images Plus; BRIAN MITCHELL/Corbis Documentary; SDI Productions/E+; antadi1332/iStock/Getty Images Plus; Irina_Strelnikova/iStock/Getty Images Plus; **U3:** Imagenavi; Ned Frisk; Uwe krejci/DigitalVision; Explora_2005/iStock/Getty Images Plus; Juzant/Digital vision; John Keeble/Moment; Mint Images RF; Grenme/iStock/Getty Images Plus; Ednam/iStock/Getty Images Plus; JazzIRT/E+; Creatikon Studio/iStock/Getty Images Plus; Atiati/E+; YangYin/E+; Skrow/E+; Luminis/iStock/Getty Images Plus; Siri Stafford/Digital Vision; Westend 61; Bonnie Tarpey - Wronski/EyeEM; Bobbieo/iStock/Getty Images Plus; Gabe Palmer/The Image Bank; Antagain/E+; Kevin trimmer/Moment; Peter Dazeley/The Image Bank; Brizmaker/iStock/Getty Images Plus; Martin Poole/The Image bank; Carolyn Hebbard/Moment Open; Asya_mix/iStock/Getty Images Plus; Lubushka/iStock/Getty Images Plus; Mai Vu/iStock/Getty Images Plus; antadi1332/iStock/Getty Images Plus; Irina_Strelnikova/iStock/Getty Images Plus; **U4:** FatCamera/E+; SwellMedia/UppercutImages; Petercade/Stone; ThomasBarwick/DigitalVision; ArielSkelley/DigitalVision; Amstockphoto/iStock/GettyImagesPlus; JillFormer/Photographer'schoiceRF; PongnatheeKluaythong/EyeEm; CSquaredStudios/Photodisc; Barcin/iStock/GettyImagesPlus; KinzieRiehm/ImageSource; PeterTitmuss/UniversalImagesGroup; DennisLane; SamEdwards/OJOImages; emholk/E+; HMVart/E+; TimClayton-Corbis; Asya_mix/iStock/Getty Images Plus; Lubushka/iStock/Getty Images Plus; Mai Vu/iStock/Getty Images Plus; antadi1332/iStock/Getty Images Plus; Kohei Hara/DigitalVision; Irina_Strelnikova/iStock/Getty Images Plus; **U5:** ViewStock; BraunS/E+; JoseLuisPelaezInc/DigitalVision; Fuse/Corbis; lisegagne/E+; MarkDouet/TheImageBank; Cirilopoeta/E+; thenakedsnail/Moment; CaseyHillPhoto/E+; Tomekbudujedomek/Moment; RichardT.Nowitz/TheImageBank; oxygen/Moment; MassimoPizzotti/Photographer's Choice RF; AlexanderSorokopud/Moment; TimHall/Cultura; LittleBee80/iStock/GettyImagesPlus; Westend61; Prostock-Studio/iStock/GettyImagesPlus; Hiroshi Higuchi/The Image Bank; AleksandarNakic/E+; Asya_mix/iStock/Getty Images Plus; Lubushka/iStock/Getty Images Plus; Mai Vu/iStock/Getty Images Plus; antadi1332/iStock/Getty Images Plus; MsMoloko/iStock/Getty Images Plus; **U6:** Image Source; NWphotoguy/E+; Wavebreakmedia; Foodcollection; Peter Dazeley/Photodisc; artisteer/iStock/Getty Images Plus; Brian Macdonald/DigitalVision; HandmadePictures/iStock/Getty Images Plus; bombuscreative/iStock/Getty Images Plus; margouillatphotos/iStock/Getty Images Plus; Rani Sr Prasiththi/EyeEm; Matt Walford/Cultura; Lisa Barnes/Moment; The Picture Pantry/Alloy; ViewStock; FGorgun/iStock/Getty Images Plus; gangnavigator/iStock/Getty Images Plus; Petra Matjasic/EyeEm; Tetra Images; Zen Rial/Moment; Bloxsome Photography/Moment; byryo/iStock/Getty Images Plus; Asya_mix/iStock/Getty Images Plus; Lubushka/iStock/Getty Images Plus; Mai Vu/iStock/Getty Images Plus; antadi1332/iStock/Getty Images Plus; Irina_Strelnikova/iStock/Getty Images Plus; **U7:** Peter Unger/Stone; Vicki Jauron, Babylon and Beyond Photography/Moment; Mike Hill/Stone; Tatsiana Volskaya/Moment; Vera Buerkle/EyeEm; avi11/E+; Theo Allofs/Stockbyte; Nneka Mckay/EyeEm; Peter Groenendijk/robertharding; Aditya Singh; kuritafsheen/RooM; Brand X Pictures/Photodisc; Mikel Cornejo/EyeEm; Xuanyu Han/Moment; vusta/E+; DaddyBit/iStock/Getty Images Plus; GlobalP/iStock/Getty Images Plus; Brian Hagiwara/The Image Bank; Martin Harvey/The Image Bank; George Doyle & Ciaran Griffin/Stockbyte; Yuxin Xiao/500px; Eve Livesey/Moment; SG Wildlife Photography/500px; StuPorts/iStock/Getty Images Plus; Vivian Yeong/EyeEm; Manoj Shah/Photodisc; Manoj Shah/Stone; Sir Francis Canker Photography/Moment; Asya_mix/iStock/Getty Images Plus; Lubushka/iStock/Getty Images Plus; Mai Vu/iStock/Getty Images Plus; antadi1332/iStock/Getty Images Plus; Simon Phelps Photography/Moment; Irina_Strelnikova/iStock/Getty Images Plus; **U8:** Neumann & Rodtmann/The Image Bank; sarayut Thaneerat/Moment; Eskay Lim/EyeEm; temmuzcan/iStock/Getty Images Plus; Paula French/EyeEm; mikroman6/Moment; temmuzcan/E+; Studio Light and Shade/iStock/Getty Images Plus; taketan/Moment; Westend61; Liliboas/E+; Richard Sharrocks/Moment; AtlasStudio/iStock/Getty Images Plus; ihorga/iStock/Getty Images Plus; EHStock/iStock/Getty Images Plus; akepong/iStock/Getty Images Plus; Richard Clark/The Image Bank; Libby Hipkins/Moment; Yanuar Sudrajat/EyeEm; ClarkandCompany/iStock/Getty Images Plus; Tetsuya Tanooka/Aflo; Rachel Weill/UpperCut Images; Stefan Cristian Cioata/Moment; Kate Kunz/Corbis; Freer Law/iStock/Getty Images Plus; Matteo Colombo/Moment; tunart/E+; Ohmega1982/iStock/Getty Images Plus; Rolfo Brenner/EyeEm; Gail Shotlander/Moment; docksnflipflops/iStock/Getty Images Plus; Kameleon007/iStock/Getty Images Plus; FotografiaBasica/E+; Asya_mix/iStock/Getty Images Plus; Lubushka/iStock/Getty Images Plus; Nicolae Gherasim/EyeEm; Mai Vu/iStock/Getty Images Plus; antadi1332/iStock/Getty Images Plus; Irina_Strelnikova/iStock/Getty Images Plus; **U9:** Bruno De Hogues/Stockbyte; Morsa Images/DigitalVision; JohnnyGreig/E+; stoonn/iStock/Getty Images Plus; SCI_InDy/iStock/Getty Images Plus; Dina Alfasi/EyeEm; Sally Anscombe/DigitalVision; levente bodo/Moment; Massimo Borchi/Atlantide Phototravel/Corbis Documentary; Andrew Peacock/Stone; Ljupco/iStock/Getty Images Plus; Fridholm, Jakob; londoneye/iStock/Getty Images Plus; C Squared Studios/Photodisc; YinYang/iStock/Getty Images Plus; 4x6/E+; mediaphotos/E+; stockvisual/iStock/Getty Images Plus; amstockphoto/iStock/Getty Images Plus; Tetra Images/Brand X Pictures; AnthonyRosenberg/iStock/Getty Images Plus; Fuse/Corbis; Ariel Skelley/DigitalVision; Vlad Fishman/Moment; Asya_mix/iStock/Getty Images Plus; Lubushka/iStock/Getty Images Plus; Mai Vu/iStock/Getty Images Plus; Irina_Strelnikova/iStock/Getty Images Plus; Hispanolistic/E+ antadi1332/iStock/Getty Images Plus; SDI Productions/E+; Maskot; Aaron Foster/DigitalVision.

Illustrations

Amy Zhing; Beatriz Castro; Begoña Corbalán; Dean Gray; Louise Forshaw and Collaborate Agency artists.

Cover illustration by Collaborate Agency.

① Me! (Page 8)

② My day (Page 20)

③ My home (Page 32)

 My sports (Page 46)

 My free time (Page 58)

 My food (Page 70)

 My food (Page 70)

 Animals (Page 84)

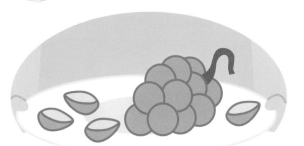

⑧ Plants (Page 96)

⑨ My town (Page 108)